# Rothe\ ob der Tauber

## GUIDE
### with 154 colour prints

*The Jakobskirche (Saint Jacob's Church) and Rooftops as Seen from the North Wall of the City (ca. 1920), oil painting by Arthur Wasse (1854-1930).*

Text: Wolfgang Kootz

Photos: Willi Sauer

## Willi Sauer Verlag

# Dear visitor,

It is hoped that this brochure will inspire you to take a walk through this well-preserved medieval town. The tours described have been proposed by the Rothenburg tourist office. First, we lead you to the main sights from Rothenburg's history as a free imperial city and provide you with a wealth of interesting information. This tour lasts approximately 2 hours, excluding visits inside buildings. In addition to this, we also recommend the paths along the oldest town fortifications - with the Klostergarten and Burggasse, lasting approximately one hour - and along the preserved city wall, which lasts around two hours. In addition, from April to December, the town offers its visitors guided tours in German and English. The evening tour with the night watchman is particularly romantic, when all the major buildings are illuminated. However, people who want to discover the true Rothenburg should avoid the main routes and explore the quiet alleys and corners, where they will discover many old houses, courtyards and fountains. The many museums and churches invite you to admire the rich cultural inheritance of the old free imperial city, and not just on wet days. In Rothenburg, bad weather can be overcome in many other ways: the Wehrgang (sentry walk) is roofed over for 2.5 km between the Klingenbastei (Klingen bastion) and the Kobolzeller Tor (Kobolzell

Gate), the "Frankenfreizeit" indoor swimming pool also offers a sauna and bowl-ing alley, and last but not least, the pleasant cafés and restaurants offer Franconian hospitality and local specialities, ranging from "snowballs" to traditional snacks with famous Franconian wine in the typical flagon-shaped bottle.

Once the rain has stopped, Rothenburg is the starting point for walks through the parks and rambles, the most beautiful of which - through the Taubertal (Tauber valley) - is described in more detail in our guidebook. Longer hikes can be undertaken in the Frankenhöhe national park, and excursions take tourists along the "Romantic Route" and the "Castle Route", which cross in Rothenburg. Excursion ideas, brochures and maps can be obtained from the tourist office, together with the current programme of cultural events. Further opportunities for an active holiday are offered by the heated woodland swiming pool, the archery and riding clubs, the tennis club and the flying club, not forgetting the river Tauber for fishing enthusiasts.

For those who wish to get to know Rothenburg and its inhabitants, we recommend that you plan to stay at least one week. There is a whole range of accommodation to choose from, from top-class international hotels to cosy guest houses. Rothenburg trips for groups and individuals lasting between 3 and 7 days can

*View of the market square: the double town hall building and the "Jagstheimerhaus" (Jagstheim House) mark the beginning of Herrngasse.*

be arranged, which saves the visitor from planning his own activities. There are plenty of reasons for and ways of visiting this medieval jewel. We hope that you will enjoy this book and your stay in romantic Rothenburg.

# History of the Town

ca. 970  The East Franconian Earl Reinger sets up the parish in the district now known as Detwang. He builds the Comburg castle near Schwäbisch Hall and the Grafenburg on the promontory above the river Tauber (hence the name, "ob der Tauber").

1108  The Earl of Rothenburg's line dies out. Earl Heinrich bequeaths all his possessions, including the Rothenburg castle, to the monastery at Comburg. This gift is not upheld by Emperor Heinrich V.

1116  The Emperor bestows Rothenburg on his nephew, Duke Konrad of Swabia, which thus passes into the possession of the Hohenstaufen family.

1137  Konrad becomes King of Germany (Konrad III) and holds court in Rothenburg. He has the Reichsburg built and allows his bailiffs to run Grafenburg.

1152  Upon Konrad's death, his son Friedrich, the "child of Rothenburg", is just 8 years old, so his cousin, Friedrich Barbarossa, is crowned king.

1157  Konrad's son Friedrich is knighted in Würzburg at the age of just 13. Friedrich I Barbarossa bestows on him the honour of Duke of Rothenburg and grants him Swabia and East Franconia.Friedrich the "Fair" holds glittering court in Rothenburg and marries a daughter of Richard the Lionheart.

1167  Friedrich the Fair moves to Italy with his cousin, Friedrich Barbarossa, to banish Pope Alexander III. The army is victorious, but a plague breaks out amongst the knights, to which Friedrich the Fair also falls victim. Friedrich Barbarossa succeeds him and allows his Franconian properties to be ruled by bailiffs.

1172  Rothenburg is granted the town charter. The first town wall is built, of which the Weißer Turm (White Tower), Markusturm (Markus Tower) and Röderbogen (Röder Arch) still remain.

1204  The fortifications are barely complete when the town becomes too large for them. The town commences construction of a second fortification which today is still largely preserved. The Kobolzeller Tor, Siebersturm (Siebers Tower), the Röderturm (Röder Tower),

Rotenburg 1648

| | |
|---|---|
| | Würzburger Tor (Würzburg Gate) and the Klingentor (Klingen Gate) are built. This first town expansion triples the area of the town and extends the fortification ring from 1400 m to 2400 m. |
| 1250 | The foundation stone is laid for the Gothic town hall (Rathaus). |
| 1251 | Emperor Konrad IV mortgages Rothenburg to Gottfried von Hohenlohe, but the town is able to buy itself free, and again in 1325 and 1349. |
| 1274 | Rothenburg becomes a free imperial city. |
| 1311 | Construction of St. Jacob's Church commences (inaugurated in 1484). |
| 1339 | Emperor Ludwig the Bavarian grants the town the right to form its own independent alliances. |
| 1352 | Rothenburg becomes independent from the empire and blood justice. |
| 1356 | An earthquake de-stroys the entire fortifications apart from a few remains. The double bridge over the Tauber is built. |
| 14th C. | The town is granted approval by Emperor Albrecht I to include the Spital district within its walls. With this second extension to the city, the defence line is increased to 3400 m. |
| ca. 1400 | The city experiences a new heyday under lord mayor Heinrich Toppler, officer general of the cities of Ulm, Nördlingen and Dinkelsbühl. He has the Chapel of St. Blaise re-built, and builds the Wildbad and the Toppler castle in the Tauber valley as a summer residence, where the controversial King Wenzel (1378-1400) is often a guest. The ancient feud with the Nuremberg Duke Friedrich ends in the devastation of the land around Rothenburg and an unfavourable peace treaty for Rothenburg (1408). In the same year, letters from Toppler to the de-posed Wenzel fall into the hands of the new King, Ruprecht von der Pfalz. Toppler is arrested on suspicion of conspiracy and locked in the dungeon under the town hall together with his eldest son and his cousin, where Toppler dies three months later; his relatives are pardoned. |
| 1450 | The end of the feuds with the princes, and the alliance of cities is forced to disband. |
| 1455 | The craftsmen of Rothenburg demand representation on the Council. |

| | |
|---|---|
| 1501 | The east wing of the Gothic Town Hall is completely de-stroyed by fire. |
| 1520 | The Jews are driven out of the city, and their synagogue and cemetery destroyed. They had already been re-located from their original residence in 1350 to their first syn-agogue and then to what is now known as Kapellenplatz in the Judengasse ("Jewry"). |
| 1525 | The "iconoclast" Dr. Karlstadt incites the millers, who destroy the valuable fixtures of the Kobolzeller Church. The town allies itself to the peasants' leader, Florian Geyers, and is defeated by the Swabian alliance. On 30th June, Margrave Casimir von Ansbach holds a trial against the ringleaders at the Rothenburg Market Square and has 17 of them publically decapitated. Only Dr. Karlstadt man-ages to flee from the city in time. The city is forced to pay war reparations. After just a few years of Evange-lism, the holy mass is re-introduced. |
| 1552 | Margrave Albrecht von Brandenburg-Kulmbach forces the city to join the Schmalkalden Alliance against the Emperor. The Margrave is defeated. Rothenburg is forced to surrender and pay enormous war reparations of 80,000 guilders. |
| 1554 | The main church finally becomes Protestant. |
| 1572 | Under the guidance of the Rothenburg architect Leonhard Weidmann, the city commences construction of the new Town Hall, followed by the "Gymnasium" (grammar school), the "Spitalbastei" (Spital Bastion), the "Baumeisterhaus" (Master Builder's House) and the "Hegereiterhaus". Numerous fountains and the Roßmühle (Nag's Mill) are intended to provide the people with water and bread even during times of war. |
| 1608 | The Evangelical princes and cities join to form the Union. |
| 1618 | The Union meets in Rothenburg. The beginning of the Thirty Years' War. The city participates in the costs and is forced to accommodate troops passing through and provide them with winter quarters. Plundering hordes inflict severe damage on the villages. |
| 1631 | Gustav-Adolf of Sweden stays in Rothenburg, leaving behind a small garrison. The request of the Emperor's commander, Tilly for winter quarters is rejected, and the townspeople occupy the defence units. After a short, energetic counter-attack, the people of Rothenburg are forced to surrender, having cost the enemy 300 lives. According to legend, the so-called "Meistertrunk" (Master Draught) saves the town from plundering and destruc-tion. Yet again, it is forced to pay high reparations. |

| 1632 | Tilly leaves the city, and later Gustav-Adolf returns with his troops. |
|---|---|
| 1634 | The Emperor's commander Piccolomini occupies Rothenburg. |
| 1645 | The city is besieged and attacked, and eventually taken by French troops under General Turenne. |
| 1647 | An army lead by the Prince and Margrave von Durlach oppresses the inhabitants |
| 1648 | When peace is declared, the impoverished town is forced once again to pay 50,000 guilders in war reparations, which it has to borrow. |
| 1650 | The last soldiers finally leave the city, which has lost half of its inhabitants due to the ravages of war and epidem-ics. It is reduced to the insignificance of a small country town, and development is suspended for centuries. |
| 1802 | Rothenburg loses its independence and is annexed to Bavaria. |
| 19th cent. | General discovery of the city for tourism. |
| | The Jakobskirche is renovated. |
| 1873 | Rothenburg becomes accessible by rail. |
| 1881 | First performance of the historical pageant "Der Meistertrunk". |
| 1898 | Founding of the "Old Rothenburg" society, which is concerned |

with preserving local history and maintaining the appearance of the city.

| 1945 | Forty percent of the city is destroyed by a bombing raid on the 31st of March. The city escapes total destruction thanks to the energetic intervention of a US general. In the ensuing years, it is rebuilt in the old style. Financial support from within Germany and abroad permits complete reconstruction of the destroyed fortifications. |
|---|---|

# 1 | Starting point for the tour
The Market Square (Marktplatz)

Ever since it was built, the market square has formed the pulsating centre of the town. As well as being the location of the weekly market, it serves as a meeting point for the locals, whilst for tourists it is the starting point for a guided tour, for the historic Shepherds' Dance and the "entry of the emperor's troops" in the pageant play the "Meistertrunk". One can pause for a moment on the steps of the Town Hall and enjoy the view of the venerable fa-cades of the houses surrounding the square. Every hour

abrupt silence when the two bull's eye windows to the right and left of the town clock open. The audience gazes spellbound at the key scene of the historical "**Meistertrunk**": former mayor Nusch is draining an enormous tankard containing three and a quarter litres of Franconian wine, whilst the Emperor's General Tilly nods in amazement. In doing so, the town mayor is said to have saved the town from destruction on 31 October 1631. Nusch is said to have spent three days sleeping off the the salvationary drink, but oth-

*The artistic clock on the gable of the Ratsherrntrinkstube (City Councillors' Tavern) with the "master draught" scene. In the centre, the old town clock, dated 1683.*

on the hour between 11 am and 3 pm and at 9 and 10 pm the town is brimming with life, but there is an

erwise suffered no ill-effects (see Calendar of Events).
It is a fact that the women and chil-

*Town Hall and City Councillors' Tavern.*

dren of Rothenburg begged Tilly for mercy here in the square on 31st October 1631. During the Thirty Years' War, the free imperial city with its largely Protestant population sympathized with the Union, the alliance of Evangelical princes and cities. In September 1631, Swedish cavalry had been accommodated in the town and a small garrison was left behind. The Emperor's General then appeared at the gates of Rothenburg and demanded winter quarters in the town, which the people flatly refused. For 2 days they defended the town bitterly, in the course of which 2 citizens and 300 attackers were killed. However, when the powder supplies near the Klingenbastei exploded and the city ran out of ammunition, the people of Rothenburg surrendered to the enemy.

The following year, the market place was once again the centre of events, when the army of the King of Sweden, Gustav-Adolf, camped here. He himself slept in the Town Hall. The square experienced its most gruesome event on 30th June 1525: Margrave Casimir von Ansbach held a trial against inciters who rioted in the recent Peasants' War. He had 17 of them publicly beheaded and ordered that their corpses should remain in the square until evening, "so that blood ran in rivulets down Schmiedgasse". A more joyful occasion took place in 1474, when Emperor Friedrich II, seated on a throne in front of the "**Ratsherrn-trinkstube**", bestowed Holstein upon Christian, King of Denmark, in a festive ceremony. This magnificent building (1446) was only accessible

9

to the city councillors. The town's justice scales were kept in its hall-like ground floor, which now houses the Tourist Information Office. In addition to the famous art clock (1910), the gable is also decorated by the large city clock (1683), which includes a calendar, the 1768 sun dial and the imperial coat of arms the double eagle with the symbol of Rothenburg.

# 2 | The Town Hall (Rathaus)

This impressive building truly dominates the market place with its magnificent **Renaissance facade**. Under the guidance of the local architect Leonhard Weidmann, one of the most imposing buildings of this epoch to be found north of the Alps was erected here in 1572-78. Formerly, this was the site of a double **Gothic building** (from 1250), as illustrated by the artist Friedrich Herlin on one of the panels on the main altar in the church of St. Jacob. Whilst the western part

*The court docks, now in the foyer of the Town Hall.*

with its slender bell tower has been preserved to this day, the eastern part fell victim to a fire in 1501. With the aid of the simple stair tower and the high corner oriel windows, the architect succeeded in breaking up the severe horizontal lines of the rows of windows and ledges, producing a harmonious combination of the two architectural styles. Even the **Baroque arcade**, which was not added until 1681, is by no means incongruous. Its round arches are decorated with the coats of arms of the electoral princes. An elegantly curved staircase leads us into the spacious vestibule of the first

*Relief (14th cent.) in the Imperial Hall.*

*View from the arcade porch of the Town Hall over the market square and its magnificent patrician homes.*

floor with its heavy beamed ceiling. The coats of arms of famous Rothenburg patrician families, such as Nusch, von Staudt, Bezold and Winterbach, decorate the walls on both sides of the magnificent portal. A painting portrays Rothenburg's most significant politician, mayor Heinrich Toppler, dressed in knight's armour. There is a bronze plaque in memory of the Swedish king, Gustav-Adolf. The famous military leader stayed here in October 1632, just a few weeks before the decisive battle in Lützen, which ended in both victory and death for him.

Behind the middle door is the **Kaisersaal (Imperial Hall)**, one of the most impressive German Gothic rooms in existence. A magnificent high wooden ceiling spans the lengthy room, which was decorated with just a few stone sculptures: the relief (14th century) portraying the Last Judgement, the window seats, the balustrade and the court barriers (all 16th century, L. Weidmann).

The likewise spacious landing on the 2nd floor is far less intricately decorated, but the magnificent tracery on the ceiling of the staircase tower with the coats of arms of the town, the empire and the 7 electoral princes and the monogram of the architect Leonhard Weidmann, are nevertheless impressive. Via the top storey, we can climb the narrow, steep entrance to the 52 m high **tower gallery**, the lofty heights of which offer a wonderful view of the medieval town with its gabled skyline and the surrounding area.

## 3 Art exhibition in the former "Meat and Dance House" (Fleisch- und Tanzhaus)

Opposite the Town Hall sparkles the most beautiful of the town's numerous fountains, **Georgsbrunnen (St. George's Fountain)**. Due to the town's plateau location, the digging of wells was both essential and time-consuming, because the water had to be piped over long distances from the neighbouring mountain ranges. Moreover, the location of these pipelines was kept secret, in order to prevent the water supply from being cut off in case of siege. The Herterichsbrunnen was already supplying water in 1446; its stonework was rebuilt in the Late Renaissance style in 1608. It is 8 m deep and, with a capacity of 100,000 litres, served as a water reserve in case of fire. The slender central column with its coats of arms is crowned by the statue of St. George - complete with dragon. In former times, the symbols of Medieval instruments of jurisdiction were set up in front of the well: the gallows, the pillory and the hoisted cage. Once a year, the shepherds danced around the well

*The impressive facades of the former Meat and Dance Hall - behind St. George's Fountain – and the Jagstheim House. On the right, the town hall oriel window.*

*The picturesque St. George's Fountain, otherwise known as Herterichs Well, flanked by Jagstheim house and the Gothic town hall with its 60 metre high tower.*

to banish the plague from Rothenburg. This tradition is still upheld in the Market Square (see calendar of events).

Two steep **half-timbered gables** complement the Herterichtsbrunnen. The decorative one with the picturesque oriel was built for mayor Jagstheimer in 1488. Emperor Maximilian I, the most prominent of the numerous noble guests, stayed there in 1513. The house, which is now privately owned, has a scenic courtyard with richly ornamented gallery balustrades, and is said to be one of Rothenburg's most beautiful patrician houses.

The "**Meat and Dance House**" next door was built on the foundations of the town's oldest Town Hall, which fell victim to a fire in 1240. Until the 18th century, the lowest floor, which now houses exhibitions of works by Rothenburg's numerous artists, was a market where butchers sold their wares. In the large room above the arches, the people of Rothenburg used to celebrate their festive occasions.

## 4 Historiengewölbe (Historical Archway) and Dungeons

After looking at the sloping facade of the Town Hall, whose only decoration is two shields, we enter the **inner courtyard** which separates the two buildings. The official measurements used in Medieval Rothenburg are proclaimed on both sides of the

*Renaissance portal in the courtyard of the Town Hall*

portal, the rod (3.93 m), the foot (30 cm), the yard (59cm) and the fathom (1.93 m). The inner courtyard is dominated by the splendid **Renaissance portal**, likewise the work of Weidmann. Until the completion of the newer section of the Town Hall in the 16th century this was the principal entrance to the building. There used to be 14 fire-proof arches on both sides, some of which were used as curiosity shops. Some of them today form the '**Historical Archways'**, displaying exhibits and scenes from the Thirty Years' War.

A staircase leads down from the Historical Archways to the **dungeons**, where many a prisoner was once made to talk in the torture chamber without any of their screams being heard from outside. The prisoner would then have to starve, perhaps for years, in one of the three cramped, pitchdark cells, as in the case of Rothenburg's most famous mayor, Heinrich Toppler. He was once captain of the region as far as Ulm, and in addition to being enormously wealthy, he also had good relations with King Wenzel, who was deposed in 1400, and sent to the Papal See. One day, secret letters

*Historical arches: scene from the Thirty Years' War*

from Toppler to ex-King Wenzel fell into the hands of the opposing King Ruprecht von der Pfalz, revealing that Toppler was interested in Wenzel's reinstatement. Shortly afterwards, on 6 April 1408, the council had him arrested and incarcerated in the foremost of the three dungeons, together with his eldest son Jakob and his cousin. Whilst the deposed mayor died after three months of imprisonment, or perhaps he was executed, his two relatives were set free a short time later after friends petitioned for their release. His successors were forced to leave the town for ever and sell their possessions in Rothenburg. After having paid more than 10,000 guilders in fines, they fled to Nuremberg. We leave the courtyard at the opposite end and approach the main church of St. Jacob, but first turn right in front of it.

*Information*

*Historical Arches:*
*15th March-30th April 10am to 4pm. May– October 9:30 am – 5.30 pm.*
*During the christmas Market 1.00 pm – 7.00 pm. Sat.+ Sun. 10am.- 4 pm.*
*January – February closed.*

# 5 The old Grammar School (Gymnasium)

The open square was once the town's church courtyard. The stone stairway opposite the east chancel is reminiscent of the Michaelskappelle (St. Michael's Chapel), to which it once be-longed. This was built as a cemetery chapel in 1449, an ornate, octagonal structure which was considered the most beautiful house of wor-ship in the town. It was for this chapel that Riemenschneider created the elaborate holy cross altar, which has been housed in the village church of Detwang since 1653. The chapel was demolished in 1804. Only the former sacristy with its attractive tracery remains. On the north side of the church square is the imposing Renaissance building of the **old grammar school** (1589), which today houses a community centre. The eight-sided staircase tower with its bulbous dome, the sun dials and above all the splendid portals, are most impressive.

# 6 St. Jacob's Church

We now turn to face the main church, whose magnificent **facade** in the high Gothic style dominates the skyline. This style is characterized by tall, narrow windows, narrow pillars and tall steeples with open helm roofs. It is noticeable that the helm roofs are of different thicknesses. According to legend, the south tower was erected by the master himself, and the more slender north tower by his apprentice. Enraged that his apprentice's work was better than his own, the master is said to have thrown himself from his tower and was killed. It is interesting to note that construction of the church lasted over a century, from 1311 until its inauguration in 1484. The Knights of the German Order commissioned the enormous building, but it was financed from the "gifts, advice, aid and joint alms of our citizens and other pious Christians, as is the custom in our country", according to the chronicle. This magnificent house of worship was an admirable achievement for the people of the time, and this becomes even more apparent when we go inside.

In front of the south tower, there is a scene from the Mount of Olives with original figures from the 14th and 16th centuries. Passing the richly de-cotrated "Bridal Door", we enter the church through the **south porch**.

*St. Jacob's Church:* April to October, 9.00 am to 5.15 pm; November and January to March 10 am to 12 pm and 2 pm to 4 pm, December 10 am – 17 pm. www.rothenburgtauber-evangelisch.de

*In the Middle Ages, St. Jacob's Church, together with the Town Hall, formed the centre of the Free Imperial City. This church, which was built during the height of the Gothic era and took more than 150 years to complete, was once Rothenburg's main house of worship.*

The overall impression created by the high aisles divided by vertical pillars is to direct our gaze upwards to God. The second impression from the nave directs us towards the slender east chancel with its tall, coloured windows between the white walls. The citizens of Rothenburg have left a unique wealth of artistic objects in this church. We follow the **southern aisle** from the gallery towards the east chancel. The bequest ranges from a depiction of the prophet Elias to the Sporlin Chapel - with a late Gothic figure of the Virgin Mary - to the Toppler chapel, a statue of St. Jacobus and the famous Hornburg epitaph, to the Altar of the Crowning of the Virgin Mary at the end. This work of art (c. 1520) is thought to be from the Riemenschneider School, and was originally displayed in the church of the Holy Spirit Hospital. It depicts the crowning of Mary, and on the side wings the Virgin with child and St. Anne (Anne, Mary and Christ was a popular combination of figures during the Middle Ages), and in the predella, Mary's death. Four impressive sculptures adorn the eastern pillar of the nave: those of St. Christopher, St. George, John the Baptist and St. John the Divine.

Three steps and the statues of St. Peter and St. Michael mark the entrance to the **east chancel**, the oldest part of the church. The magnificent choir stalls were built by a Rothenburg architect in 1514 for member Knights of the German Order. The paintings above them portray former principal preachers in this church from the era following the reformation. The east chancel is dominated by the gloriously colourful **altar of the Twelve Apostles**, one of the most valuable historic treasures in Germany. It was financed by generous gifts on the part of Heinrich Toppler; the paintings are the work of the famous artist Friedrich Herlin from Nördlingen. The magnificent sculptures in the shrine were carved Swabian masters: to the left of the impressive crucifix are the Virgin Mary, St. Jacob, the patron of the church, and St. Elizabeth, and on the right, St. John, St. Leonard and St. Anthony. The scene on the predella - Christ and his twelve disciples - gave the altar its name. The paintings on the front of the altar wings portray scenes from the life of the Virgin Mary: to the right there is the Annunciation and the Visitation of the Blessed Virgin Mary, below it the Birth of Christ and the Circumcision, and to the right the Worship of the Three Kings and a scene in the Temple and, on two of the pieces, Mary's death.

On the backs of the panels, Herlin portrayed the death of **St. Jacob** and his **legend**. The correct sequence of pictures is produced if one imagines the altar wings closed:

The saint is taken prisoner while teaching (picture ❶), executed ❷ and his corpse taken to a medieval town ❸. This is followed by scenes from the legend of St. Jacobus: pilgrims on their way to St. Jacob's grave are dining in an inn, whilst the

*St. Jacob's Church: the main altar (Altar of the Twelve Apostles), in addition to the appealing carved figures in the shrine, also contains magnificent paintings by Friedrich Herlin (15th century).*

landlord is secretly putting a golden beaker into one of their travel bags ❹. The land-lord reports the theft of his beaker to the authorities and it is found in the baggage of one of the pilgrims. In order to protect his father, the son of one of the pilgrims confesses to the theft and is hanged ❺. The mourning father finds his son still alive at the gallows, because St. Jacob has spared him. Together with the judge, they return to the inn ❻. When the landlord hears the news, he disbelievingly claims that the young man is as dead as the chickens on his spit. However, the chickens fly away, proving the pilgrim's innocence ❼. After being taken down from the gallows, the son accompanies his father home. The wicked landlord, however, is lead away to the gallows ❽. Picture ❸ of the corpse being taken away portrays one of the oldest true-to-life

19

*Details from paintings by Friedrich Herlin.*

*St. Jacob's Church: detail from a painting on the back of the right-hand altar wing portrays the market square and the town hall prior to the disastrous fire in 1501.*

portrayals of a city in the Middle Ages and depicts Rothenburg's market square in the 15th century with the full double Gothic town hall. The front part, which was burnt down in 1501, is fronted by curiosity shops. The rear part with the slender tower has been largely preserved, as has the Ratsherrentrinkstube (City Councillors' Tavern), with its half-timbered upper floors, and the towers of St. Jacob's Church. However, the town gate in the rear right has disappeared. The 17 metre high window at the end of the chancel contains some valuable **stained-glass window paintings** from circa 1400 which are dedicated

to Christ's redemption (right) and the life of the Blessed Virgin (left). The lighter central window, which dates from the year 1350, shows scenes from the life and passion of Christ surrounded by depictions of the apostles. The sacrament niche on the north side at the same height as the altar dates from the same century. Above this, there is an exquisite masonry sculpture of God the Father sitting on a throne, surrounded by the Lord of Sorrows and Mary, as well as John the Baptist and John the Evangelist. Coats of arms above the rear wall of the northern choir stall are reminders of the patrician families as an acknowledgement for

21

*St. Jacob's Church: sacrament house, which once contained the host.*

their generosity to the Church.

The **Franciscan altar** at the front of the north aisle was formerly housed in the Franciscan church, for which it was carved by the famous Tilman Riemenschneider in circa 1490. The shrine contains a sculpture of a sleeping monk and St. Francis of Assisi receiving stigmata. The reliefs on the altar wings portray scenes of martyrdom, whilst at the foot of the altar the Virgin Mary is depicted with baby Jesus, surrounded by people praying.

We pass the first pillar, likewise decorated by four apostolic figures, and the second, which supports the New Gothic chancel (1854). Further epitaphs and statues and two chapels decorate the north side of the chancel. Looking up, we can see the **west gallery**, where the current **organ** was dedicated in 1968. Experts through-

*Louis de Toulouse altar circa 1490 AD, by T. Riemenschneider.*

*St. Jacob's Church: view of the east chancel.*

out the world have praised is fullness of tone. 69 registers and 5500 pipes are operated from two consoles with a total of 6 keyboards; the numerous recitals are a delight for the ears of all lovers of organ music (these take place twice a week in the summer). Whereas the preceding instrument had stood in the centre of the gallery for four hundred years, this new organ made space for the most precious work of art in the church, the Holy **Blood Altar**. It was produced between 1499 and 1505 in the

*St. Jacob's Church: The Holy Blood Altar with its famous relic in the gold-plated cross was the destination of numerous pilgrims in the Middle Ages.*

*St. Jacob's Church: the main picture with the portrayal of the Last Supper is thought to be one of Tilman Riemenschneider's greatest masterpieces. In the centre of the picture is Judas, handing Christ the bread.*

workshops of the Rothenburg cabinet maker, Erhard Harschner, and the sculptor Tilman Riemenschneider, who produced all the figures and the reliefs. It was commissioned by the Rothenburg Town Council in order to provide a worthy setting for a treasured relic in the Middle Ages: a capsule of rock crystal said by tradition to contain 3 drops of Christ's blood, which is embedded in the gold-plated cross (c. 1270) above the shrine and which gave the unique work of art its name. The portrayal of the main picture, the scene of the Last Supper, is particularly impressive. It demonstrates the genial artist's extraordinary powers of expression, and is one of his greatest works. The distribution of the characters in this depiction is unusual: it is not Christ who stands in the centre, but Judas the traitor. Jesus is offering him a portion of bread and saying, "One of you will betray me". The effect of these words is reflected in the faces of the disciples: consternation, agitation and helplessness. Only John, Christ's

*Holy Blood Altar: Scenes from the life of Jesus (entry into Jerusalem, Last Supper, Mount of Olives).*

favourite disciple, is sleeping peacefully at his master's breast. The open lattice work between the pillars of the shrine, together with the light centre windows of the galley, lend the main picture a unique impression of space. The shrine is supported by a delicate structure, with the high vault above it; both are adorned with ornate figures. The artistic reliefs on the wings of the former Pilgrimage Altar portrays Christ's entry into Jerusalem and the scene at the Mount of Olives: Jesus is praying, the disciples are sleeping, and in the background, Judas is entering the garden followed by the henchmen. The entire sculpture is carved from lime-wood and was originally coated with egg white to which the artists had added ochre and black for pigmentation. After leaving the magnificent house of worship, we bear to the right and follow the Klingengassse, which takes us underneath the galley of the church. We soon come across one of the quaintest oriel windows in the town, the picturesque **"Feuerleinserker"** (c. 1600). We turn left into the Imperial City Museum (Reichsstadtmuseum) in the former Dominican Priory.

*The oriel window "Feuerleinserker", and passage underneath the galley of St. Jakob's Church.*

# 7 | The Imperial City Museum

In 1258, nuns from the neighbouring priory of Neusitz moved to Rothenburg after the Master of the Imperial Kitchens, Lupold von Nordenberg, bequeathed his estate to them. Until its dissolution in 1544, it was inhabited by the unmarried daughters of the local patricians and the landed gentry. Their generous contributions enabled the buildings to be converted and extended, including the erection of the spacious priory church (1270), which was demolished in 1813, whilst at the same time, the All Saints Altar by the sculptor Tilman Riemenschneider disappeared without a trace. Numerous parts of the buildings were changed over the centuries. Since 1936, however, the former priory has been used as the **Imperial City Museum**. Visitors are fascinated by the historical rooms: the priory

*Historical kitchen in the Medieval Dominican Priory (founded in 1258), now part of the Imperial City Museum.*

*Imperial City Museum: Klosterhof 5, 91541 Rothenburg o.d.T.: April through October, 10:00 AM – 5:00 PM; November through March, 1:00 PM - 4:00 PM. Phone 09861/939043 Fax 935206. Email: reichsstadt-museum@rothenburg.de, www.reichsstadtmuseum.rothenburg.de*

*Kurfürstenhumpen, glass painted with enamel, 1616.*

*Cup of the Rothenburg Retailers' Guild, 1687.*

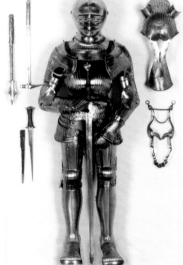

*Maximillian armour, ca. 1525, from the Baumann Collection.*

31

*Imperial City Museum:*
*Part of Rothenburg Passion by Martinus Schwarz (c. 1450 – c. 1510) "Pontius Pilatus washing his hands", tempera on wood, 1494.*

living rooms, bedrooms and work rooms with their beamed ceilings (14th century), the convent (15th century) with its artistic wooden barrel-vaulting, the festive hall with its coloured ceiling (18th century), the herb kitchen and above all, the **old priory kitchen** (c. 1300), thought to be the oldest preserved kitchen in Germany. The local authorities have been careful to ensure that the rooms are not overloaded with exhibits. These include the magnificent early Gothic cloister which provides a stylish setting for the "Rothenburg Passion", a cycle of twelve paintings depicting scenes from Christ's passion, painted in 1494 by Martinus Schwarz. In addition to furniture, household ware, workmen's tools, agricultural equipment and arms dating from various centuries, the original "**Elector's Tankard**" is on display

dating from the year 1616, which held 3 1/4 litres of wine and which was used for presenting welcoming drinks to visiting dignitaries. This tankard is the theme of the legendary "Meistertrunk", performed every year in the historic pageant.

The museum gallery is proud of its comprehensive collection of works by the English painter **Arthur Wasse** (1854-1930), whose impressive paintings capture the various moods of Rothenburg's numerous romantic corners. After living and working here for many years, his widow bequeathed his art collection to the town.

Back in the Klingengasse, we follow it north. The next crossroads marks the end of the oldest fortification. The Judengasse on the right once housed the members of Rothenburg's Jewish community, until their expulsion in 1520.

## 8 | Klingentor (Klingen Gate) and St. Wolfgang's Church

The route to the 30-metre high **Klingenturm (Klingen Tower)** (13th cent.), with its corner turrets and sentimental lantern hood, attention is immediately drawn to the small, towerless **St. Wolfgang's Church**, which is joined to the outer gate tower. The two later Gothic

*Defence wall at Klingen Gate. The gate tower is particularly attractive, with its ornate oriel windows and decorative lantern covers.*

shows how the old part of the city has expanded. Since the 16th century, when large copper water tanks were installed, the gate tower has served as a water reservoir supplying the town's wells. In the bastion in front of the tower (c. 1500), our windows are decorated with ornate tracery, whilst the third window is undecorated, because this corner contains the entrance to the gallery and gate tower. A few steps beyond the outer gate, the connection between the church and the defences

*Entry to the defence wall at Klingen Gate*

The upper of these shows the course of the defences running between the outer gate tower and the adjacent artillery rampart within the church wall. Underneath the church floor were casemates from which the defendants could fire on any attackers who had managed to penetrate the dry moat. This shows that the house of worship was planned as a fortress church from the outset. Even the chancel and sacristy are provided with defences.

The present-day stone bridge was originally made of wood, and the town half could be pulled up if necessary, providing additional reinforcement for the outer gate.

becomes even more apparent: the northern wall of the church consists of enormous square blocks, interupted only by two rows of embrasures.

It is worth **visiting** this interesting **building**, both for the attractive al-

*St. Wolfgang's Church, otherwise known as the Shepherds' Church, was built as a defence inside Klingen Bastion. On the left it is joined to the outer gate of the fortifications.*

*St. Wolfgang's Church: from left to right the Holy Virgin Altar, the St. Wolfgang's Altar and the Wendelin Altar.*

tars and for the defences. The church was erected towards the end of the 15th century on the spot where, according to legend, local shepherds used to pray to the patron saint Wolfgang to protect them from the jaws of wolves. He is depicted on a relief between the church doors and at the centre of the **main altar**, flanked by St. Sebastian and St. Rochus. The paintings on the altar wings, as well as those on the wings of the altar of the Holy Virgin, are the work of the Rothenburg painter Wilhlem Ziegler and date from circa 1515. They portray scenes from the lives of the three saints. In addition to St. Wolfgang, St. Wendelin was also a popular patron of the rural population, and the church's third altar is dedicated to him; note the fine fan vault.

At the main altar, stone steps lead down through the thick northern wall to the casemates below the church. The gate tower with its picturesque observation post is reached via a spiral staircase to the left of the entrance. Today, it is furnished as a **shepherds' dance chamber**.

**St. Wolfgang's Church:**
*April through September 10 AM – 1 PM and 2.30 PM – 5 PM; October, Christmas Market weekend, and Dec. 25th – Jan. 6th 11 AM – 4 PM. Closed Tuesdays. November and January till March closed.*

The sentry walk in the northern wall connects the gate tower to the artillery ramparts laid in the 16th century, providing an effective strategic position for shooting on the area in front of the long northern flank of the city wall.

After leaving the inner gate tower, we turn right and go **outside the wall** to the round Strafturm (Punishment Tower), a former prison. Following the path below the city wall, it becomes apparent why Rothenburg was never attacked from this angle, especially as the steep slopes were kept artificially bare for tactical reasons. There are many unexpected views of the Tauber valley with the village of Detwang, the half-hidden mills and the Hohenloher plain.

*St. Wolfgang's Church: stairs leading down to the case mates.*

A memorial plaque on one of the houses provides information about how the infamous "iconoclast" Dr. Karlstadt was rescued. In 1525, one of his supporters lowered him out of the window here in a basket, enabling him to avoid the fate of the remaining protagonists, who were decapitated on 30th June 1525 in Rothenburg Market Square.

*Klingen Bastion: Shepherds' Dance Chamber*

36

*The castle gate is decorated with the coats of arms of the city and the empire, and on the right, on the outer gate, is the coat of arms of the Dukes of Rothenburg and Comburg.*

 ## The Burgtor (Castle Gate)

We enter the site of the castle, now converted to gardens (Burggarten), via a side portal. On the left is the tallest **gate tower** in the town. After the castles were destroyed in 1356 by an earthquake, this gate became essential, and was erected immediately in the years that followed. The outer gate with its coats of arms and guard house and customs house with their pointed gables were added prior to 1600. On the middle gate, the openings for the drawbridge chains can still be seen, together with the mask from whose mouth hot pitch could be poured onto attackers. A so-called needle-eye in the inner gate wing enabled individuals to be let in without the sentries having to open the entire door. During the hours of darkness when the city gates were closed, people were only allowed to leave and enter with the express approval of the council.

## 10 The Castle Gardens

The middle path leads to the only large building in the well-kept gardens. The Duke of Rothenburg's castle once stood on the protruding rock overhang. In spite of the earthquake in 1356, the old castle keep was preserved until 1282, but was then demolished, and now, old pictures and documents are the only reminders of the castle. After the Duke's family line died out in 1108, the powerful Hohenstaufen family acquired ownership of the castle. They had a much bigger building, the "Imperial Castle", built in the front part of what is today the castle gardens. Under its protection, a flourishing community of servants and craftsman developed between the 12th and 14th centuries. At the beginning

*The relief in the shrine of the Franciscan altar portrays St. Francis of Assist receiving stigmata and was carved by T. Riemenschneider.*

of the 15th century it covered an area of 400 square metres and had a total population of 20,000, distributed throughout the city and 167 estate villages. Only one building from the former imperial castle survived the earthquakes, at least in part, thought to be the keep. In circa 1400, mayor Toppler had the ruins re-built and decorated with wall paintings. The "**great house of the Dukes**", as the building is still known, today serves as a memorial for the soldiers who died in the two world wars. The enormous stone slabs are the final remaining witnesses to castle architecture in the Staufen period at the height of the Romanesque era in Rothenburg. The remains of the other buildings of both castles were used by the local people to build houses and defences.

Turning left in front of the chapel, we enjoy a magnificent **view of the southern part of the town** with the distant Stöberleinsturm, the Kobolzell Kirchlein ("Little Church"), the enormous double bridge and the water mills, 24 of which once belonged to Rothenburg. We then curve round to return to the castle gate and re-enter the city.

*Franciscan Church: The Franciscus Altar.*

# 11 The Franciscan Church (Franziskanerkirche)

Immediately behind the gate is the "**Puppet Theatre for Adults**" in **Herrngasse**.

It forms a direct connection between the former castle and the centre of the town, the market square. The broad street was once home to the highest class of servants at the castle, who later became the patrician class, the town nobility, who governed Rothenburg's fate for centuries. One of their prerogatives was to be allowed to hold a horse and cattle market, which gave the street its second name, "Herrenmarkt" (gentry market). Almost all the proud patrician houses have their gable sides facing the street. If you look up, you will see a beam projecting from the gable end. When fitted with a pulley, these were used to hoist up supplies for storage in the loft. According to the regulations of the time, all households were obliged to store sufficient grain supplies for two years in case of war.

The simple **church** on the right-hand side, consecrated in 1309, belonged to the mendicant order **of Francis-** **cans** who settled in Rothenburg in 1281. Interestingly, the wooden division, known as a "Lettner", between the monks' gallery and the seating area for laymen, has been preserved. The pictures, a sequence of Christ's Passions, date from the time when the basilica was built. Numerous tombstones and memorials of local patrician families and the neighbouring landed gentry are found on the floor, walls and pillars. The most noteworthy of these are the **epitaphs** for Hans von Beulendorf and his spouse, Dietrich von Berlichingen, the grandfather of the famous "knight with the iron fist" and the Rothenburg captain Peter Creglinger. The intricately carved

*The broad Herrngasse was once the favourite residential street of the town nobility. In the middle, the attractive Herrnbrunnen fountain.*

*Forged iron signs in Herrngasse*

main altar portraying the stigmatisation of St. Francis of Assisi, the founder of the order, is now displayed in the main church .Unfortunately, it is no longer possible to visit the interesting interior of the early Gothic church. The Franciscan monastery was disbanded in 1544, and many of its buildings were destroyed in the 19th century.

Finely-wrought iron window bars (1722) in the Baroque style decorate the attractive **von Staudt house** no. 18 opposite the Franciscan church. Inscriptions proclaim that various prominent guests once stayed in this building: Emperor Charles V and Ferdinand I, his brother and successor, as well as Gustav-Adolf's queen, Marie Eleonore von Brandenburg. It is well worth visiting the staircase tower with its impressive wooden staircase and romantic courtyard, arguably the most beautiful in Rothenburg. Pillars, galleries, oriel windows and a staircase

tower represent the entire range of medieval design possibilities for a "house in the open-air", as was then popular amongst the town nobility. The von Staudt family, who lived there for 4 centuries, had the building rebuilt in the old style following a fire in 1687. The courtyard can be visited for a charge. Other patrician houses can be seen at numbers 11, 13 and 15.

Water supply has always been one of the city's main problems. The geographical situation on a plateau made it almost impossible to dig deep wells. Hence, in the 16th century, a reservoir was built by installing a copper tank in the upper part of the Klingen Gate tower. It was fed via pipes from neighbouring mountain ridges and supplied the numerous pipe wells in the town, including the neat "**Herrenbrunnen**" (**Gentry Well**) in the middle of the street, which reflects the tasteful wealth of the local residents.

Over the last twenty years, Rothenburg's Herrngasse right next to the

*Stairway leading to the German Christmas Museum.*

market square has become a meeting place for connoisseurs of German Christmas traditions. Käthe Wohlfahrt's **"Christmas Village"**, which is open year round and is quartered in five patrician houses that have been connected with one another, offers more than fifty thousand Christmas items: Christmas tree ornaments, nutcrackers, and incense burners, as well as Christmas pyramids and musical clocks from the Erz Mountains. The atmospheric decorations include a five-metre

high Christmas tree in the middle of a snow-covered Franconian market square, a nutcracker that is nearly four metres tall, and a five-metre high Christmas pyramid.

The upper storey of the house is home to the **German Christmas Museum**. Here visitors can steep themselves in the history of German

*Selection from the collection: "Historical Santa Claus".*

Christmas traditions in 250 square metres of exhibits covering everything from the origins of Christmas tree ornaments during the Biedermeier period up to the early fifties of the last century.

---

**German Christmas Museum:** *Open April – Mid January 10:00 AM – 5:00 PM, Mid January – March only Sat., Sun. 11:00 AM – 4:00 PM closed on Good Friday. Opend on Christmas Day and Boxing Day. www.weihnachtsmuseum.de*

*Santa Claus with Sleigh
(1920/1940)*

*Flying illuminated angel, Schneeberg
Room, second half of the 19th cen.*

Christmas as celebrated by our parents and grandparents comes alive here in the form of more than five thousand exhibits in the Wohlfahrt Collection, as well as exhibits that are permanently on loan from international collectors. Tree ornaments made of a very wide variety of materials, Christmas tree stands, Father Christmas figures, Christmas cards, paper crèches, advent calendars, nutcrackers, Christmas pyramids, incense burners, lighted angels and spiders, exhibited in a "heavenly" atmosphere, enchant visitors and revive childhood Christmas memories in the ten exhibition rooms.

*An indoor view of Käthe Wolfahrt's Christmas Village.*

## 13 The Doll and Toy Museum

At Herterichsbrunnen (Herterichs Well), the picturesque Hofbronnengasse leads to the **doll and toy museum**, containing over 600 German and French dolls from the past 200 years.

The exhibits include doll's houses, doll's rooms, doll's kitchens and shops, fitted with all the charming objects needed for a complete doll's household, as well as puppet theatres, railways, metal toys, wagons, toy farms, school and carousels, hand-carved wooden toys and thousands of charming accessories from a bygone childhood.

45

A tour of the museum offers the visitor far more than just a nostalgic journey through time.

Many cultural and social aspects are portrayed in the exhibition, because a child's puppet world reflects the grown-up's world in miniature, thereby providing an excellent source for discovering our ancestors' lifestyles.

← *Doll with dog*

*Large and small doll* →

*Doll's school* ↓

↑ *Doll's kitchen*

← *On the merry-go-round*

**Doll and Toy Museum:**
*Open March through December 9:30 AM – 6:00 PM; January/ February 11:00 AM – 5:00 PM. Hofbronnenstraße 11-13. Phone 09861/73 30, Fax 86748, www.spielzeugmuseum-rothenburg.de*

The street **Obere Schmiedgasse**, which we will follow toward the south part of the city, begins at the market square. There one immediately notices the richly ornamented Renaissance façade of the **Master Builder's House**, which was the home and studio of stonemason Leonhard Weidmann. Dragon-shaped volutes soften the formal rigidity of the terraced gable. The lintels of the two upper stories show alternating depictions of the seven virtues and the seven vices, such as kindness and gluttony, motherliness, and fraud (bottom row, l. – r.). This house, which is probably Rothenburg's loveliest patrician residence, was built in 1596 for the then Master Builder of the City and demonstrates both the wealth and tastefully culti-vated living of the time. Today it is used as a café, whereby guests can admire the still cosy inner courtyard with the magnificent wooden bal-ustrades, the bull's eye windows, and the galleries. In 1400, the at-tached guest house "zum Greifen" was the property and **residence of Lord Mayor Toppler**, and already an inn. As legend would have it, Mrs. Toppler tried to dig a tunnel from here to the gaol in which her husband and her oldest son were incarcerated. The plain gable was replaced in the 17th century.

*Master Builder's House in Schmiedgasse: window supports portraying the 7 virtues and the 7 sins of the Middle Ages.*

# *Old Iron Craftship*

# 14 | The Medieval Crime Museum

The **Burggasse** on the right is undoubtedly the oldest and one of the most romantic streets in Rothenburg. At the entrance to the **museum**, which is housed in the former Commander of the Order of St. John, is a ducking stool for bakers whose bread was too light. The only law enforcement museum in Europe depicts a unique and comprehensive insight into 1000 years of legal history up until the 19th century, covering four storeys and an area of 2000 square metres. With commentaries which everyone can understand, objects and documents depict the nature of court proceedings and torture, punishment and legal folklore. In addition, significant laws and ordinances, medals and seals, documents, illustrations, caricatures and much more have been collected and displayed under the impressive wooden ceilings or in the cellar vaults of the former seminary. Whilst the visitor will shudder at the numerous instruments of torture and execution, he will also grin at the implications of the masks of disgrace and throat vices and wonder about the educational effect of these crude punishments.

*Museum of crime: Vaulted cellar roof of the former commandery of the Order of St. John, with torture instruments and methods of punishment.*

**Crime Museum:**
*January, February and November 2:00 PM-4:00 PM. March and December 10:00 AM-4:00 PM; April-October 9:30 AM – 6:00 PM Phone 09861/5359 Fax 8258 – www.kriminalmuseum.rothenburg.de*

**Civil punishment**

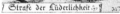

*Civil punishment in the 17th/18th century. Top row, from left to right: quarrelsome women – a poor musician is denounced – a baker is ducked for baking bread which is too light. Centre: Walking with the drinker's barrel – a cheat at the pillory. Bottom: Punishment für wicked women – for rude comments or jokes – forced labour as a public punishment.*

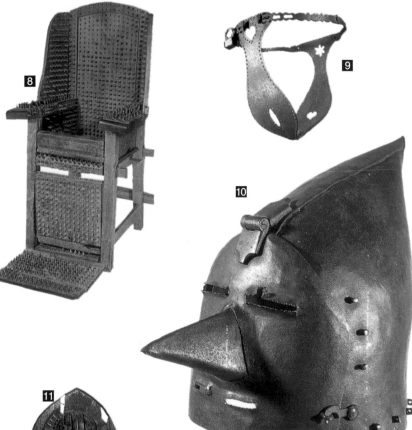

*Museum of crime:* **1** *Neck violin for quarrelsome women,* **2** *mask of disgrace with trunk and* **3** *für men who have behaved like animals.* **4** *Drinker's barrel* **5** *-Mask of disgrave for gossiping women and* **6** *for men.* **7** *Flute of disgrace for poor musicians.* **8** *Interrogation seat for witch trials.,* **9** *Chastity belt.* **10** *Executioner's mask.* **11** *The iron virgin, a coat of disgrace and punishment for sinful women und girls.*

53

*View through Schmiedgasse towards the City Councillors' Tavern. Artistic signs in front of the shops and guest houses decorate the facades.*

## 15 St.-Johannis-Kirche (St. John's Church)

The **church** (1390-1410) once belonged to the hospital next door, and when it was built, parts of the superfluous southern gate of the oldest town fortification were incorporated in the building. For example, the gate hinges on the gable side of the church once belonged to the old "St. John's Gate". The row of houses opposite was erected in place of the oldest town wall, and the road in front is still called "Alter Stadtgraben", or Old Moat.

The "Roter Hahn" restaurant was once the **residence of Mayor Nusch**, the hero of the "Meistertrunk" legend. A memorial plaque in Latin recalls this salvatory act. On 19/20 September 1532, King Gustav Adolf of Sweden stayed here with

## 16 Plönlein ("Little Square") and Siebersturm (Siebers Tower)

Intricate wrought iron signs on restaurants and shops are evidence of the craftsmanship tradition which gave Schmiedgasse (Smithy's Lane) its name. We are soon standing in front of one of the most famous sights in the town, the street fork known as "**Plönlein**" (from the Latin word "planum" meaning flat square). A charming, narrow, half-timbered house with a well is framed by the Kobolzell Gate and the taller **Siebers Tower**, and to the left and right, lovingly renovated town houses. Both gate towers were built during the first extension to the town (from 1204). The Siebers Tower with its solid square slabs formed the southern entrance to the town before the Spital quarter was included inside the fortifi-cation.

*The Siebersturm tower (13th century as seen from the Spitalviertel Kappenzipfel).*

*View from "Plönlein" towards Siebers Tower (on the left) and the tower of*

*Kobolzell Gate, secured the entrance to the town.*

## 17 The Kobolzell Gate

Immediately behind the Siebers Tower, a narrow street with steps leads down to the **Kobolzell Gate** and its long, rectangular bastion. From the inner tower, we follow a staircase up to the "Steige", the steep road leading up from the Tauber valley. Inside the bastion, it is easy to imagine the difficulties one could cause an attacker from this vantage point. A sentry and customs' house is adjacent to the archway of the outer gate, which is decorated on the outside with ornate coats of arms. Presumably because of the sloping ground, the builders positioned the tower next to the entrance instead of above it. From the inner gate tower, it is possible to climb onto the **battlement walk** and the crenellated "**Devil's Pulpit**", which functioned as a look-out.

*The outer gate of Kobolzell Bastion with its coats of arms, with Kohlturm (on the right) and Kobolzell Gate Tower, and above it, Siebers Tower.*

*Nag's Mill was driven by horses and acted as a substitute for the mills in the Tauber valley in times of war and drought.*

## 18 Rossmühle ("Nag's Mill")

Above the bastion, we follow the town wall, past the Fischturm, to an open square with the remains of a 400-year-old lime tree. It is dominated by the solid **Rossmühle** with its tall flying buttresses. In the Middle Ages, the people were forced to store grain supplies in their houses for 2 years in order to be prepared in case of emergency or war. In the case of a siege, or if the water levels were extremely low, the numerous mills in the Tauber valley could not be relied upon, and hence Rothenburg built this **town mill** (1516) for such eventualities. Inside, 16 horses drove the 4 grinding wheels. Today, the spacious building is Rothenburg's second youth hostel. Opposite it is an enormous **tithe barn**, which once served to store the town's share of the farmers' harvest.

Passing between it and the battlements, we reach the building complex of the **Heilig-Geist-Spital (Hospital of the Holy Spirit)**, which gave the entire district its name: Spital quarter, also known locally as the "pointed hat" due to its shape.

*The picturesque Hegereiter-haus in the middle of Spital Courtyard.*

*Spital Courtyard: cellar and bakery with the covered well.*

# 19 The "Hegereiterhaus".

In the middle of the courtyard, surrounded by plain utility buildings, is the charming **Hegereiterhaus** (16th century), yet another impressive building by the architect Weidmann. Its pointed tent roof and the narrow, spiral staircase tower with its decorative lantern-like turret provides a charming contrast to the sober buildings surrounding it. The ground floor once housed the hospital kitchen, whilst the upper storey provided accommodation for the administrators of the extensive hospital properties. The house's name is misleading, because the "Hegereiter" was actually an employee of the imperial city who was responsible for Rothenburg's villages and estates.

The **Spital** was built in 1280 from a donation and was situated outside of the city wall at that time. It was particularly concerned with care of the poor and the sick, and provided accommodation for travellers who reached the city after dark, when the gates were locked. Numerous donations extended the property, which was managed from the large building whose gable side faces the Hegereiterhaus. Likewise built by Weidmann, it served as a hospital until 1948; today, it is an old people's home. To the left of it is the dainty **church**, the only building remaining from the founding years of the Spital. Inside the single-aisle church there are a number of precious statues and interesting epitaphs dating from the 14th and 15th century and an interesting sacrament house (c. 1390).

The courtyard is closed on the northern side by a building complex with the "**Pesthaus**" or plague annexe - cell-like isolation rooms for patients with contagious diseases - and the half-timbered building of the cellar and bakery, which is now a youth hostel. The former **well** is covered with an ornate iron trellis.

*Fortifications at Stöberleins Tower, and adjacent to this, the gable of the Imperial City Festival Hall.*

## 20 | Imperial City Festival Hall (Reichstadthalle)

Directly adjacent to the legendary **Stöberleinsturm** with its oriel windows, the impressive former **Spital tithe barn** (1699) forms the left-hand side of the complex. In 1975, the town had it converted to the Imperial City Festival Hall. It can now accommodate up to 600 people in the hall alone, offering an historic setting for congresses, meetings and other events. At the south eastern corner, we pass the former administrative building and leave the Holy Spirit Hospital, and approach the southern town gate.

*View through the outer gate to the fortified Spital Bastion, Rothenburg's mightiest and most modern bulwark.*

## 21 | The Spital Bation (Spitalbastei)

In order to do justice to this youngest and most imposing **bulwark** of the city fortification, we recommend walking through the deep dry moat and along the **walkway** within the walls.

Leonhard Weidmann built the double bulwark in the form of an eight, with 7 gates, portcullises, and a drawbridge. Above the defiant stone slabs, he had a walkway built, along which sentries could ride. The inscription on the key stone on the outer gate arch bears the date 1586, together with Weidmann's initials and a Latin inscription, "Peace to

*Flower garden in Spitalgasse.*

those who enter, farewell to those who leave". Next to it there is an old customs house and a watch tower. An adventure playground on the moat bed provides children and adults an opportunity to rest; a second playground can be found by the Würzburg Gate.

*View from Röder Tower along the city walls with Hohenner Tower, the ornate Sulpur Tower and the impressive Rotten Tower.*

From the gate tower, we climb up to the **sentry walk**, offering magnificent views through the arrow slits, looking down on angular courtyards and narrow roofs. When our path abruptly changes direction, we pass

**The ornamental gable of the Old Forge in front of the Röder Gate. From the top floor, visitors can enjoy a magnificent view.**

from the "pointed cap" quarter into the fortifications of the first town expansion. This area of the fortifications was heavily damaged by an intensive air raid in 1945. Its reconstruction was financed primarily by donations from both Germany and abroad. **Inscriptions** with the names of the donors can be found on the fortifications. We soon pass the round **"Faulturm" ("Rotten Tower")**. Its enormous height was necessary to provide an adequate view of the land below. According to legend, it is as deep as it is high, and many a prisoner wasted away here, leaving behind his putrefied remains - hence the name "Rotten Tower".

Shortly afterwoods, we catch a glimpse of one of the most charming half-timbered buildings in the town - the **Gerlachschmiede**. Above the open courtyard is a decorative, slender gable with attractive windows and brightly coloured coats of arms.

*View through the outer gate into the Röder Bastion.*

At the next gate tower, the **Röder-tor**, we leave the sentry walk and circle the bastion. The main gate is flanked by two attractive guard-rooms and customs houses with pointed roofs and firing slits both inside and outside. A wooden bridge leads across the walled moat to the outer gate of the square bastion with its sentry walk.

Leading to the inner gate there is a second moat which is crossed by a bridge, half of which is a drawbridge which could be used to reinforce the front gate in case of defence. The outer ward directly in front of the

inner gate was roofed, and its towers offered effective defence against any attackers who had managed to penetrate the outer ward. The **main tower** (13th cenury) represents the oldest part of this gate structure, apart from the half-timbered upper storey, which was added at a later date. It affords a magnificent panoramic view of the western fortifications and the roofs in the old part of the city. The **tower room** contains an exhibition of documents and pictures from 1945 when this area of the town in particular was destroyed extensively.

*View from the Röder Tower towards the town centre.*

71

*Flowers in bloom at the Röder fountain. Between the attractive half-timber facades, you can see the Röder Arch with the sturdy Markus Tower.*

## 24 Markusturm (Markus Tower) and Röderboden (Röder Arch)

We now follow the Rödergasse into the town. The attractive town houses and the romantic **Röder fountain**, together with the Röder arch and the imposing hipped roof of the Markus Tower, form an over-whelming ensemble. The two defences dated from the 12th century and were part of the first town fortification.

## 25 Old Rothenburg's Craftsmen's House

If you wish, you can turn left into the old moat from the Röder Arch and visit **Old Rothenburg's Craftsmen's House**, no. 26. Built at the end of the 13th century, this was home to a wide range of craftsmen over the course of 700 years. There is evidence of coopers, lead-black

*Craftsmen's house: cobbler's workshop*

dyers, weavers, shoemakers, tinkers, potters, basket-weavers, soapboilers, pavers, tin-founders and masons. For many years, the house was inhabited by a hermit who shunned the modern world, and required neither running water nor electricity. Accordingly, this jewel of a medieval building was preserved virtually unaltered. Eleven rooms and small chambers with low ceilings are furnished in the style of centuries

past; the journeyman's room has the original sleeping accommodation, the kitchen has an open fire, and the living room is furnished with the irregularly shaped oven tiles produced in the 14th century on a potter's wheel. Even today, the 14 metre deep well inside the house could still supply its inhabitants with water.

Passing through the **Röder Arch** with its spear-shaped tower, we enter the oldest area of the city. Adjacent to the sturdy **Markus Tower** is the **bailiff's house** with its barred windows. It was used as a prison until the 18th century, and now houses the city archives.

*Bedroom and nursery*

*Craftsmen's House:*
*Easter Weekend - October 31st Mon-Fri 11.00 am–5.00 pm.*
*Sat.+Sun. 10.00 am–5.00 pm. Nov. 1st-Jan. 7th 2.00 pm – 4.00 pm.*
*January 1st - Easter closed.*

Passing in front of the bailiff's house, we follow the course of the first city wall, across the Milchmarkt (Milk **Market**) to **Kapellenplatz (Chapel Square)** with the "Seelbrunnen" well. Until 1804, the Chapel of St. Mary (Marienkapelle) stood here, which until the end of the 14th century had been the synagogue of the city's 500-strong Jewish community. It was here that the famous and influential Rabbi Meir ben Barruch worked (c. 1215-1293). When the synagogue was converted, the Jews were brusquely moved into the Judengasse (Jews' Lane) outside of

*Markus Tower with the Röder Arch and "Büttelhaus" (former town prison).* →

← *White Tower and attractive hotel facade in Georgengasse*

the city wall. A new synaogue was built in the Schrannenplatz area, near the Jewish cemetery, until the Jews were banished completely from Rothenburg in 1520. The cemetery and synagogue were demolished later, and now the **Jew's Dance Hall** (Judentanzhaus) next to the White Tower is the only reminder of the former community. Once the social centre of the persecuted minority,

it was later used as a shelter for the poor or "Seelhaus" ("Soul House"). The outside of the attractive half-timber structure is decorated by a picturesque oriel window. The short path from the White Tower through Georgengasse to the Market Square emphasizes once again the narrowness of the confines of the first city walls.

## Tour of the first city wall

For this interesting route of approximately 1.4 km we will need about half an hour. It follows the approximate course of the oldest town fortification. We set off from the **inner castle gate** where the

**Burggasse** branches off to the left from Herrengasse. At the city wall, the Burggasse branches off to the left again. It was formerly known as "Zur Höll" (In Hell) because it was partly overshadowed by the Francis-

77

can monastery, which made it very dark. The house in Burggasse 8 still calls itself "Zur Höll" and is thought to be the oldest residential building in Rothenburg. At Johanniskirche, the romantic lane joins **Schmiedgasse**, which we follow to the right for a short period. The houses on the left in the "old moat" were built in the 13th century when the first town wall became superfluous. The town sold the wall, including the land, to people wanting to build, and hence the semi-circular shape has been preserved to this day. Passing the Old Rothenburg Craftsmen's House (25) we come to the first preserved city gate, the Röder Arch (24) in **Rödergasse**. It was protected by the enormous Markus Tower which, in a similar manner to Kohl Tower at the Kobolzell Gate, was erected next to the city gate for safety reasons. The White Tower (26) has likewise been preserved, and was formerly an exit leading towards Würzburg. The adjacent "Jewish Dance Hall" was

*Galgengasse: White Tower with the picturesque oriel window of the Jewish Dance Hall.*

once the centre of the local Jewish community and contains tombstones belonging to members of the community on the inside of the garden wall. This marks the beginning of **Judengasse**, where the unpopular citizens were forced to move to at the end of the 14th century, before being banished from Rothenburg completely in 1520.

At **Klingengasse**, we turn off to-

↑ *Inner courtgard of the priory.*

*Idyllic view through the autumn forest to Toppler's Little Castle in the Tauber valley.* ➤

wards St. Jacob's Church and after a few metres, approach the Imperial City Museum. We cross its courtyard diagonally and enter the attractive **priory garden** at the south end of the front building. Following the city wall, we return to where we started within a few minutes.

## Tour of the fortifications

This path leads us along the 3.4 km long medieval fortifications, partly inside the wall and partly outside of it, and takes a good hour. Starting from the **Castle Gardens** (10), we leave the gardens via an **opening in the wall** near the Chapel of St. Blaise and follow the flat path south along the city wall with its scattering of towers. Running be-

*A birdseye view of the historic Old City.*

tween the oldest town wall - until the bend near the former **Johanniterkloster** - and the little river, this path offers splendid views on both sides, and is justifiably referred to as the "**Tauber Riviera**". At **Kobolzell Gate** (17) we cross the road and follow the defence wall of the **Spital district**. Next to the picturesque **Stöberleinsturm** - recognizable with its four romantic oriel windows - is the massive former **tithe barn**, now the **Imperial City Hall** (20). Passing the **Sauturm**

the "pointed hat", as it is known locally. We follow the city wall on the outside as far as the **Röder Bastion** (23), whose main bulwarks formed the gate towers with their protruding defences. If, as in this area, the distance between city gates was relatively large and the terrrain unsuitable for effective defence, heavy defence towers such as the imposing **Faulturm** were built. The ornamental, round Schwefelturm ("Sulpur Tower") and the much larger Hohenersturm, which was already within

*Spital Bastion: the powerful walkway protected the town in case of war with mobile artillery. Behind it, the Spital Gate.*

("Pig Tower"), which is slightly to one side of the wall, we reach the **Spitalbastei (Spital Bastion)** (21), the southernmost point of the city fortifications. A **break in the wall** shortly before the next tower, the "Kleiner Stern", enables us to enter the fortifications, before leaving it again near the **Siebers Tower** (16) via a road. This is also the end of the walls encompassing the second expansion to the town (14th century),

the outer ward of the Röder Bastion, were built between it and the Röder Tower. The distances between towers was calculated according to the range of crossbows, which were the most effective instrument of defence prior to the invention of fire arms. From the Röder Gate, we remain inside the wall as far as the **Klingen Gate**. Between these two bastions is the **Würzburg Gate**, which unfortunately is less well preserved.

*The Röder Gate looked very defensive to the enemy.*

Beyond it were the gallows, the reason for the gate's other name, "**Galgentor**" (Gallows Gate) (27), with "**Galgengasse**" (Gallows Lane) leading through it.

The gallows stood here as a symbol of the city's legal jurisdiction as an imperial city until the beginning of the 19th century, when the town was annexed to Bavaria.

This was the weakest point of the fortifications in case of attack, and indeed, during the Thirty Years War, Tilly (1631) and Turenne (1645) entered the city at this point. Built after the first expansion to the city (in the

*Galgentor (Würzburg Gate) with outwork.*

13th century), the gate tower was destroyed by fire during the following century and rebuilt. After 1600, it was protected by the addition of an outer ward, a broad moat and a rampart, connected with a drawbridge. In the years that followed, another bastion was erected level with the rampart, with an outer ward and outer gate, so that enemies were faced with a total of 5 gates. The stone bridge between the outer gate and the bastion could be blown up in case of attack. However, the fortifications were heavily damaged by the effects of the Thirty Years War, and they were demolished in the 19th century. Today, only the old gate tower and its outer fortifications remain, leaving little impression of the defences which once existed. The name of the next tower "**Kummereck**" ("Worry Corner") says a great deal about the problems faced by the soldiers on this side of the defence line. This is followed by **Henkersturm** and **Pulverturm**, in front of which is Schrannenplatz,

*Idyllic autumn scene at Klingen Bastion*

*The former village of Detwang in the Tauber valley is older than Rothenburg.* ➤

the grain market, and location of the Jewish cemetery and synagogue until their expulsion in 1520.

We leave the town for the last time on this tour at **Klingen Gate**. We follow the path inside the former bastion which leads first to the **Strafturm** (Prison Tower). The path on the right leads to Detwang (1.2 km), but we walk underneath the town wall, past the **Klosterturm** and the **Bettelvogtsturm** and back to the **Castle Gardens**.

## A walk through the Tauber valley

This tour contains Rothenburg's main attractions outside of the city walls: the parish church in Detwang, the Toppler Castle (Topplerschlößchen) and the double bridge with the Kobolzell Church. It is 4 km long, so you will need a good hour just to walk it. From **Prison Tower near Klingen Gate**, the path descends steeply into the valley, and within a few minutes we reach the Romanesque parish **church in Detwang** (31). The old village and its parish is older than Rothenburg. The church was built in 1170, but the interior was converted to Gothic style. The group of statues in the simple shrine of the **main altar** protrays Jesus on the cross, to the left the weeping Mary and John, and to the

right a priest and soldiers. It is the work of **Tilman Riemenschneider**, who carved it for the Michaelkapelle (St. Michael's Chapel) in Rothenburg. The reliefs on the altar wings come from the artist's school, but are not the work of the master himself. Other details worth seeing are

once supplied Rothenburg with flour are still preserved. The **Topplerschlößchen** (Toppler's Little Castle) (30) is in a quite different style. It was built in 1388 in the form of a Romanesque residential tower, as was common at the turn of the century. It was built for the famous

*Church in Detwang: View towards the east choir, the cross altar and the late gothic side altars.*

a relic cross dating from the Otto period, the Gothic sacrament house and the octagonal advent light.
We walk back a short distance, cross the Tauber and follow the path along the river. Numerous **mills** which

mayor Heinrich Toppler, who used the building as a summer residence and as a meeting place for political discussions. Toppler is said to have often received the controversial King Wenzel here, whom he continued to

---

**Parish Church of Sts. Peter and Paul**
*April – October 8:30 am – 12.00 pm and 1:30 pm – 5:00 pm (from June 1 – September 14 until 6:00 pm. November - March 10:00 am – 12.00 pm and 2:00 pm – 4:00 pm, closed Mondays.*

*Holy Cross altar: the centre group with Jesus on the Cross, the Holy Virgin and the High Priest with soldiers is the work of Tilman Riemenschneider.*

*Disciples resting at the Mount of Olives*

*Sleeping guards at Jesus' grave.*

*Toppler's Little Castle: the famous mayor's residential tower in the Tauber valley, built in the style of a castle surrounded by water*

support following his deposition in 1400, leading to the final downfall of the people of Rothenburg. The building, with its coats of arms, has been preserved in full, and furnished with furniture from the 16th-19th century. The rustic kitchen is particularly genuine.

When we walk along the bends of the Tauber, there are many charm-

**Toppler's Little Castle**
*Fri. – Sun. 1:00 – 4:00 PM and by appointment.*
*Closed November*

ing views of the old part of the town with its towered skyline and the 60 m town hall tower in the centre. From there, the tower watchmen had a wonderful panoramic view of the town to enable them to warn of the outbreak of fire or the approach of an enemy as quickly as possible. One particularly attractive picture is the enormous **double bridge** (28) in the foreground. This existed in a similar form in 1330, but was fortified in the Middle Ages, thereby forming an outer protection for the city gates.

Nearby, the roof of the towerless **Kobolzell Church** (29) peeks out of the trees. It was built in 1472-1501 in the late Gothic style and was generously furnished thanks to numerous donations, until incited millers became active as "iconoclasts" during the peasant war, and destroyed the entire contents. In the centuries that followed, it served as a store until it was recruited once again to the service of the church in 1864. Our tour takes us across the "Steige" or incline, through the **Kobolzell Gate** or the entrance near St. John's Church, and back into the old part of the town.

Of the many opportunities for rambling around the imperial city, we particularly recommend an excursion to the "**Engelsburg**", situated approximately 1.5 km above the double bridge. It was from this bare mountain that Merian painted his famous view of the town in 1648, with the Tauber and the bridge in the foreground. Remains of the **Celtic circular wall** can also be found, which was erected by the Celts as a refuge in approximately the year of Christ's birth, as protection against the advancing Teutons.

*The double bridge with the city view in the background.*

# Holiday Programmes

## Easter

In Rothenburg, the Easter season marks the start of the historic pageants: an event staged by the Historic Theatre Festival and the dancers of the Shepherds' Guild lead off the series. Organ and chamber music concerts in the Franciscan Church and St. Jacob's Church provide entertainment.

## Whitsun

The Whitsun Festival begins with the historic craftsmen's and tradesmen's market (until Monday). On Saturday, the historic "**Meisterunk**" pageant is performed for the first time, **troops in historical uniforms** parade **marshals at 3:00 PM, passing through the Old City before encamping** in front of the Würzburg Gate. On Monday, first in front of the Würzburg Gate and then at the market square, the whole city and its guests bid adieu to the historic Whitsun festival days, during which many of the citizens of Rothenburg help bring the era of the Thirty Years' War back to life.

*Festival parade in historic uniforms.*

parade through the Old City already starting at noon, and already in the morning on Sundays and Mondays. The first half of the day is taken up by **Festival performances** and performances of the **shepherds' dance**, until the **historic festival**

*Medieval City Councillors.*

*Historic field encampment in front of the Würzburg Gate* ➤

# Imperial City Festival Days

*Medieval musicians.*

On the first weekend in September, visitors to Old Rothenburg feel as if they have been transported back to the Middle Ages. On Friday evening, the historical groups march in a **torchlight procession** to the market square, where they are greeted and introduced by the Mayor. On Satur- day (starting at 2:00 PM) and Sunday (starting at 10:00 AM), citizens pres- ent **scenes from Rothenburg's past** in the alleys and on the squares of the Old City. Astounded guests admire the historic costumes and accesso- ries from seven centuries: the band of knights from 1274, the rebellious peasants of 1525, and the cattle deal- ers of the 19th century. A **fireworks gala** with Bengal lights on Saturday evening commemorates the bom- bardment of the city and its burn- ing houses. The "**Meistertrunk**" and the **shepherds' dance** are performed again on Sunday, before all the his- torical groups assemble in the late afternoon at the market square for the **closing festivities**.

# Historical Events

## The "Meistertrunk"

The traditional play was written last century by the Rothenburg craftsman and story-teller Adam Hörber. The performance is comparable to the famous Oberammergau plays. It was performed for the first time on Consecration Day in 1881, the year marking the 250th anniversary of the worst part of the Thirty Years' War. Since then, the play either directly or indirectly, in the pageant or other historical performances. Formerly, performances were restricted to Whitsun, but they are now also performed in October in the Kaisersaal of the Town Hall. The play is based on the events of 29-30 October 1631, including the legend surrounding it:

A few days previously, King

*The "Meistertrunk" historical pageant: the vintner hands Tilly the tankard with the welcoming drink.*

has been performed every year, and the number of performances is increasing continually due to popular demand. A large proportion of the local inhabitants are involved, Gustav-Adolf of Sweden left the largely Protestant town which feels beholden to him, leaving behind a small garrison. At this point, the Emperor's general Tilly, commander of the Catholic "League" arrives at the city walls with most of his troops and demands that they be let in and provided with winter quarters. The councillors decide to resist. Even the town's final contingent of young people are sent onto the defence wall, beseeching the aid of the heavenly powers. Hope and jubilation spread when messengers report that troops are approaching from a great distance, but it is not Gustav-Adolf's troops, but instead, further reinforcements for Tilly. Nevertheless, the people of Rothenburg heroically hold out against the superior forces for a further day. One group of enemy troops which has managed to penetrate the town fortifications is forced back beyond the walls. But then bad tidings are brought: the gunpowder tower has exploded, partially destroying the neighbouring Klingen bastion. Hence, further resistance is pointless, and the white flag of surrender is hoisted at the Gallows Gate. Shortly afterwords, Tilly and his companions enter the room, furious at the bitter resistance, for which four of the councillors are to be hanged. As they refuse to draw lots, he says that they will all die. Even the niece of mayor Bezold is unable to soften the heart of the general with her pleading and the cries of her two children. Bezold is sent ahead to fetch the executioner. During this time, the daughter of the cellar master offers people drinks, and her father praises his wine. Councillor Winterbach brings the enormous tankard for a welcoming

*Historical pageant: bad tidings für the city councillors*

drink, and Tilly and his followers pass it around several times. The general admires the enormous vessel, which holds 3 1/4 litres, and, somewhat more relaxed, says that he will show mercy if one of the people present is able to empty the tankard in a single draught. Former mayor Nusch, after some hesitation, accepts the challenge, and to the amazement of the people present, he succeeds. Tilly keeps his promise, and the people rejoice and sing a song of thanks, which brings the performance to a close.

In the Middle Ages, sheep-keeping and the wool trade played a significant role in the life of the town and its villages. In 1517, the local shepherds' guild was granted the right to celebrate a "Shepherds' Day" once a year with music and

# The shepherds' dance

dancing. The story goes that the shepherds succeeded in banishing the plague from Rothenburg with their dancing. Another legend tells of a shepherd who had a wonderful dream in which he found treasure and the shepherds danced for joy. On Easter Sunday and Whitsun Sunday and on several other occasions during the summer, the colourful dancing couples appear in the market square to revive this tradition. Further information can be found in the Shepherds' Dance Gallery in the guard room of St. Wolfgang's Church, otherwise known as the Shepherds' Church.

*Performance of the historical shepherds' dance at the market square before a backdrop of many spectators.*

*A scene from a farce by the Franconian shoemaker-poet Hans Sachs, one of the "Master Singers" of Nuremberg.*

## The Hans Sachs Plays

Hans Sachs, born on 5th November 1494, was a shoemaker and "master singer" in his home town of Nuremberg. Having written more than half a million lines of verse, including 208 plays, he became famous as the "shoemaker poet". Since 1921, the best of his original farces have been performed by the Rothenburg Hans Sachs Players. The mischievous Franconian sense of humour, the shoe-maker poet's lively tunes, and the faithful reproductions of costumes from the "Meistersinger" era, performed in the historical setting of the Kaisersaal in the Town Hall, make the plays a real treat for the eyes, ears and soul. All the town's festivals include these plays, which are performed nearly every Friday not only between mid-May and July, but also in September and October, as well as on many other weekends from May until October.

## The Adult Puppet Theatre at the Castle Gate (Burgtor)

The comic Heinz Köhler performs short plays full of humour, satire and irony in his puppet cabaret. Lovers of sophisticated cabaret can enjoy it every afternoon and evening for 90 minutes in a humorous programme which, nevertheless, often conceals a much deeper meaning. The Adult Puppet Theatre at the Castle Gate is open daily except Sundays from April to October and in December.

## A Winter Fairytale

At the beginning of the advent period, the town is transformed into a large Christmas market. Whilst in other towns, one is dazzled with strings of electric lights, this Medieval town is steeped in a magical atmosphere. The "Reiterlesmarkt" surrounding the Town Hall is a very special experience: there are stalls selling toys, Christmas tree decorations and Christmas tree fairies, and a delicious smell of mulled wine and Franconian Bratwurst. The market is governed by the "Reiterle" ("little horseman"), the embodiment of old customs. With

*The romantic Christmas market on the market square.*

a little snow, the "winter fairytale" is complete. Organ and brass band concerts, rides on the mail carriage, the children's torchlight procession, the Rothenburg "Sternsinger" and the "Pelzmärtl" ensure that there is never a dull moment for visitors. Occasionally, night watchmen process through the streets, sounding their horns and announcing the time. Between Christmas and the first few days of the New Year, the city and hotels offer a comprehensive programme of events with concerts, rambles and special performances with atmospheric evening entertainment and glittering New Year's Eve balls, a performance of the Hans Sachs plays, and even a "ski jumping competition for the master draught tankard".

Those who are unable to visit the "Winter fairytale" of Rothenburg at this time of the year could visit the "Christkindlmarkt" and "Christmas village" at the beginning of Herrngasse. They display an entire range of traditional German Christmas articles all year round, with a unique decoration and selection. Children and adults stand and admire the 5 m high Christmas tree surrounded by "snow-covered" Franconian half-timbered houses, the enormous Christmas pyramid and the "king of the nutcrackers", and are transported to the "winter fairytale", even in the middle of summer.

*The romantic Christmas Market before the impressive backdrop of St. Jacob's Church.*

*Advent atmosphere in front of the romantic Röder Arch.*

← *Kobolzell Gate*

*Rothenburg in winter* →

*Georg's*
↓ *Markus Tower*          *Fountain* ↓

*Am Plönlein* ↑

← *Market Square*

*Old Forge* →

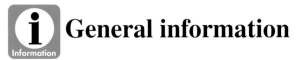 # General information

**police** (accident, robbery etc.): ☎ 110

**fire**: ☎ 112

**First Aid – Ambulance**: Bavarian
Red Cross, Galgengasse 35, ☎ 1 92 22

Tourist Office
Marktplatz 2, 91541 Rothenburg ob der Tauber,
☎ (0 98 61) 404 800, Fax ☎ (0 98 61) 404 529
www.rothenburg.de · E-Mail: info@rothenburg.de
Apr. - October: Monday - Friday 9 am–7pm.
Saturday and Sunday 10 am– 5pm.
November to March: Monday - Friday 9am. – 5pm.
Saturday 10am – 1pm..
Advent season : Saturday Sunday 10am-5pm. **Fishing**: District Fishing Association
☎ (0 98 61) 875619

**Lending Library and Reading Room**:
Klingengasse 8, ☎ (0 98 61) 933870,

**Railways**: railway station Rothenburg
(Bahnhof) ☎ (0 98 61) 4611

**Camping**: camping site at Tauberidyll
Detwang, ☎ (0 98 61) 31 77 and Tauberromantik
Detwang, ☎ (0 98 61) 61 91

**Rent-a-cycle**: Fahrradhaus Krauße.K. Wenggasse
42 Tel. 09861/3495

**Aerodrome – flights over city**: Aero-
Club, Bauerngraben, ☎ (0 98 61) 74 74

**Swimming und Sauna "Frankenfreizeit"**:
Ozone indoor swimming pool, (mid September
to mid May) and heated outdoor swimming pool
(mid May to mid September) ☎ (0 98 61) 45 65;
sauna and massage ☎ (0 98 61) 45 65; restaurant
with large terrace, bowling, ☎ (0 98 61) 39 71;
Nördlinger Straße (The Romantic Route)

**Lost property**: Rathaus-Arkaden
(Town Hall Arcade), entrance far left,
☎ (0 98 61) 404-150

**Changing money**: Possible at all banks

**Church services**: Catholic: Saturdays 06.00 am,
Sundays 10.30 am. held in the Church of St. John
(Johanniskirche); Protestant: Sundays 7.30 am and
9.30 am in the St. Jakobskirche.

**indoor swimming**: see **Frankenfreizeit**

**Youth Hostels**: Roßmühle,
Mühlacker 1, ☎ (0 98 61) 9 41 60

**Cinema**: Kapellenplatz-Lichtspiele,
Kapellenplatz 14, ☎ (0 98 61) 46 58

**Hospital**: Ansbacher Straße 131,
☎ (0 98 61) 60 21 70 70

**Old-time coach trips**: Tours of the
town as well as half-day and full-day excursions.
Further informations obtainable at the Verkehrs-
amt (tourist office).

**Museums**: Reichsstadtmuseum (Imperial
City Museum), Crime Museum furnished as in the
Middle Ages, Alt Rothenburger Handwerkerhaus
(Old Rothenburg's craftsmen's house) ,Toppler-
schlößchen (Toppler castle), Historiengewölbe
(Historical Arches), Puppenmuseum (Doll and Toy
Museum). Weihnachtsmuseum (German Christmas
Museum). Times for opening see text.

**Polizei**: ☎ (0 98 61) 97 10

**Post offices**: Bahnhof-
straße 15, Rödergasse 11

**Reichsstadthalle (Imperial City Hall)**:
Main hall seats 600 persons, also smaller room
and parking facilities,
☎ (0 98 61) 4866

**Travel agency**: Reisebüro Thürauf, Im Bahnhof,
☎ (0 98 61) 46 11, travel agency (Reisebüro) Ha-
berecker, Wenggasse 1, ☎ (0 98 61) 94840
City Reiseservice, Galgengasse 41,
☎ (0 98 61) 9 44 60

**Riding**: Reitstall am Schwanensee
(3 km away), ☎ (0 98 61) 32 62

**Sauna**: see **Frankenfreizeit**

**Small arms club**: air guns, pistols and
rifles. Open to guests an Thursdays
between 8 und 10 p.m. Schützengilde (Small
arms club), Paul-Finkler-Straße, ☎ (0 98 61) 32 77

**swimming**: see **Frankenfreizeit**

**Taxi**: ☎ (0 98 61) 95100, 44 05, 72 72, 2000

**Tennis**: to mid April daily 8 – 12 a.m.,
2 – 5 pm, tennis-club, Am Philosophenweg,
☎ (0 98 61) 78 93

**Rambling and Hiking**: A marked path
for ramblers throuth the Tauber Valley over the
Engelburg heights (which gives one a Merian Pan-
orama over the valley and Town) and also in the
wooded area of Frankenhöhe.

# Index

# Information to the map

1. Marked place
2. Town-Hall
3. Art exhibition
4. Historical vaults
5. Former High School
6. St. Jakob's Church
7. Imperial City Museum
8. Klingentor, St. Wolfgang's Church
9. Burgtor –Castle Gate
10. Burggarten – Castle garden
11. Franciscan Church
12. German Christmas Museum
13. Doll and Toy Museum
14. Medieval Crime Museum
15. St. John's Church
16. Plönlein and Siebers Tower
17. Kobolzeller Gate
18. Rossmühle – a horse-operated mill
19. Hegereiter House
20. Reichsstadthalle
21. Spital Bastion
22. Gerlachschmiede - Gerlach's forge
23. Rödertor
24. Mark's Tower and
25. Roeder Arch Old Rothenburg Craftman's Houes
26. White Tower
27. Galgengate
28. Double Bridge
29. Kobolzeller Castle
30. Toppler Castle
31. Detwang

Fuchsmühle

Hansrödermühle

Tauber

Lucas Rödermühle

Herrenmühle

Steinmühle

Mühlacker

Spitalgasse

Richtung Langenburg

Friedrich-Hörner-Weg

Spitaltor   Kinderspielplatz

auch für Wohnmobile

B 25, Romantische Straße
Dinkelsbühl – Augsburg